Memory Lane

To Slavica
Enjoy
M Westworth

Memory Lane

MARGARET WESTWORTH

To order additional copies of this book, contact:
Xlibris
1-888-795-4274
www.Xlibris.com
Orders@Xlibris.com
712397

Contents

Dedication

I dedicate this book to my children:

Sharon Ann

Margaret Ruth

Ronald Thomas

Betty-Lou

I love you all!

Acknowledgements

My family who have been very supportive. I could not have done this without them.

My granddaughter, Amy Evans, who took my picture for the jacket of the book.

Sarah Gibson, Ruth Allison and Sarah Perkins and the rest of the Xlibris team who have been so helpful.

Kick Start

You sounded down so very much
I thought I'd drop a line,
It's not what's happened
That counts so much
But what you do about it,
Things always happen for a reason
Whether it's our mistake or not,
So now is the time to pull ahead
And straighten out this mess,
Pick up yourself and carry on
With head held high and shoulders back,
You know you did your best,
Turn fate around and meet the rest
Of life's challenges head-on,
'Cause things are always happening
To try and drain our strength,
Just don't forget to keep your faith
And all will be corrected.

"Kick Start" was written for my daughter, who was going through a very bad time at work and I wanted her to feel better about herself. She told me it did help, and she was the one who named the poem, not because of what it said, but because of what it did. It was the kick that started her on the road to recovery and to fight back.

Priorities

Of all the things that one should keep
Ahead of all the others
Priorities sometimes are the cause
Of heaviness plunged deep within
Each day the trials that come
With every waking day
Makes life's ill-timed obstacles
A challenge to strengthen concentration
Required for keeping priorities
In focus every day

Change

While struggling with the changes
That lie ahead of you,
It's hard to see
How one can survive
The drastic change of pace,
For the life that was will never be,
But in its place you'll see
A different kind of way.

It's one that lets you appreciate
The little things that seem to be
Forgotten in the past.

So now is the time to plan ahead
For exactly what is needed
To satisfy your life,
And when those deep, dark spaces
Bring doubts inside your mind,
Coming forth with fears,
Keeping sharp edges on trying times,
You'll have the means to stop all that
Because you were prepared.

Memories

It's been a while since you went away
But the memories are not dim,
Although it seems the time we spent
Feels just like the other day,
They were the times, such happy times,
That brighten up each day
And chase away
The problems of today
That darken each one's way,
So now it helps my sanity
To find a place each day
To bring you back to me
And fill a few precious moments
With memories of yesterday.

"Memories" was written when my mother passed away twenty years ago, but it is much more helpful since my husband passed away two years ago. It has also helped others that I have given it to since they lost their loved ones.

Family Strain

The strain on families
When morals are forsaken
Tears deep within one's soul,
For when you've done your very best
And the trials never cease,
What questions do come forth?
They reach into the deepest depths
Of inner strength that God gave us,
But through it all you kept your faith
When others would have said
There is no God at all,
So the times ahead, all kinds of times
That test that faith again,
Will calm down because you know
That He is there
And will forever help you through
Those troubling times that seem
To constantly be with you.

Fighting Back

All troubles that have come your way
A mountain they must seem,
Surely now you realize
That it is up to you
To draw upon your inner strength,
The one God gave to you.
It matters not what others
Think of the things you do,
For others are not living
With the demons in your soul,
Life is not an easy thing,
But with determination and
The help of many others,
The benefits you'll see
Will bring such great rewards,
So now's the time to put to rest
Those demons deep inside,
And the peace that you are seeking
Will surely come your way.

Soothing Pain

Suddenly I realize
My thoughts are just reflections
Of feelings deep inside,
The awakening grasp
Does soothe the hurt
And put an end to pain.

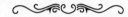

Reflection on Change

The twilight of our years gives
Perspective different views,
What once was clear and precise
Becomes jaded with passing time,
When the vitality of youth
Transposes tender years
To weathered times of lifelong practices,
You understand the change.

Changes

Time to search for a reason
To accept the changes taking place
In things you can't control.

Aim your thoughts to understanding
The past that led to the decisions
To seemingly unfulfilled dreams held dear.

Unchallenged

I look out on a world of change
And wonder what comes next,
For standards we once held dear
Are now quite incomplete,
How can we teach structure
In all we say and do
If change keeps on going
Unchallenged in any way?

My Friend

In the time I've known you
We talked about so many things
Shared each other's dreams
And were there for when
The other needed help.

Yet sometimes we pull away
Afraid to call upon
Our friendship that we both need
To strengthen the bond
That rarely comes along.

When now that we realize
What our friendship does entail
Our fears should go away, and
I know that we will always be
The friends that we are now.

This was for one of my best friends, Marjorie W. I wanted her to know how I felt. She was always there when I needed her.

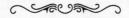

Christmas

The wonderment of Christmas
That comes at each year's end,
Brings a time for families
To gather once again.

As the years pass by
What changes we do see,
But still we carry on
Our tradition from the past.

Then with the happy times
We all appreciate,
Our memories are replenished
With thoughts of times gone by.

Just to keep as a reminder of our family get-togethers.

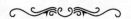

Our Christmas

With lights all twinkling on the tree
And presents 'neath the boughs
The turkey roasting fills the air
To whet one's appetite.

Ohs and ahs as each gift gives way
To excited persons waiting
All the happiness we each receive
Comes with sharing with each other.

So the sights and sounds that fill the air
As families gather for the day
Bring pleasant memories to
Who takes part in our yearly gathering.

Great memories.

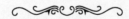

The Loss of Dad

The loss of one so close to me
Gives grief the edge it seems,
If known would distress
That person who was a gentle soul,
In time the grief will pass
And in its place an emptiness
Only time can heal.

Written to help with the grief of losing my parents. They died eighteen months apart. I took care of my mother after Dad passed away.

Missing Mom

I wonder if we talked about
The things we used to do
If it would make it easier
To stop the ache inside.

I picked up your piece of needlework
You left here by your chair,
A flood of memories came gushing forth
And stirred the ache inside.

But slowly as I pass each day,
The ache just ebbs away,
Now when I see the many things
You created lovingly,
I know the ache will slowly flow away.

I missed Mom a lot, and the poem helped with the loss.

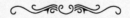

For My Mom

When I look around, I see
The things that you enjoy,
Such simple things that are
There for everyone.

The color of nature
Creates splendor successfully,
Just like the caring
My mother gave to me.

Mom was always making things, and I often thought about the things she did.

My Dad

A kind and gentle soul
As honest as could be
Who was always there for me,
His talent as a craftsmen
Was the very best,
All the things he made for us
Left treasures to hold dear,
Now when I see
Those creations sitting round
The pleasure that I get
Is one of thankfulness
Because he was my dad.

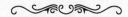

Filling Spaces

In the space that is around me
While music fills the air,
My thoughts do wander
To the departure for today,
And in that place created
A pleasant dream indeed
All weariness goes way.
So as I gain composure
While my tensions fade away,
The space that is around me
Has soothed my weary soul.

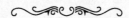

My Daydreams

I want to dream of happy times
And of an ideal life,
I want to think of days gone by
That did not have any strife,
I want to have my daydreams
Each and every day,
But then I bring myself
Down to my place on earth
And open up my eyes
To see what things go on instead.

Anorexia

Like a shadow you crept inside
To fill the corners deep within,
You drain all strength
Till none is left and so you win—
You claimed my soul.

Now that you own me, body and soul
I'll tell you what I feel,
The image that haunts each day
A mirror on the wall
Is always so revolting.

You anger me, but fight back I can't
My mind you do control,
The concentration has gone from me
And fear is ever present
Each and every day.

My insides you twist about
And turn them inside out,
You churn and churn till eventually
A skeleton is what's left
With death just steps away.

My friends and family
You've tried to take
With your relentless grip,
This course I live, you gave to me
Is one that I regret.

l

l

l

I've put my family through enough
With all my temperament,
I decided a while ago
To take back my control and rid myself
Of this disease called Anorexia.

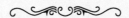

Facing Facts

The time has come
To face the facts
That build your temperament
So helpful in our world,
Always giving of yourself
To ease the load of others,
Rarely taking time away
For pleasures you enjoy,
How pleasant it would be
If just a few should
Care as much as you.

If I Could

It tears apart
My heart to see
The terror that is felt
So suddenly, from out of the blue.
And if I could, I would
The terror fade away,
But each must handle
In one's own way
The terror that haunts the soul.

It tears apart
My heart to see
The hurt that you are feeling
And can do naught about it.
For if I could, I would
The hurt just wipe away,
But each must handle
In one's own way
The hurt that haunts the soul.

Life's Highway

As we travel down life's highway
In this great land of ours,
We must pause and think about
How fortunate we are,
For where else in this troubled world
Is living made as easy,
While in so many other places
Life's so very harsh?

Without the basics we enjoy
A difference we would find,
And when we start to question
Why our life is filled with woe,
We need to take a look at
The less fortunate than we
And be thankful to live in
This great land of ours.

Quitter I won't be

Disappointment is so strong
I wonder what to do,
Will I give in and
Call it quits, or
Fight it to the end?
But when I sit and think
Which way is best for me,
The truth jumps out
And hits me in the eye,
The message that has come
Through all the distress
That seems to plague my life
Is a quitter I won't be,
No matter what gets in my way,
I'll try to handle all that comes
With great determination
To make those things come right.

Grace

We need to thank
The Lord above
For all that He's created,
There is so much
That He has given
To grace our life
Here on this earth,
So thank you, God,
For giving us
The strength we have
And blessing us
With Your great love.

Colors of Mood

Colors come in many moods
And range from dark to light,
With all our feelings affected by
A circumstance or deed,
One's mood can be adjusted
By color that surrounds
The things that are occurring,
Letting our mood be altered
By color that's around.

Cherish

Cherish the time
That's given to you
To make the most
Of things held dear,
When one of you departs
Into the great unknown,
What else can replace
Those things that made
Our time that came from
A smile, a gift, a touch
So special to hold,
Making the time
That's given to you
More precious than before.

"Cherish"—I felt such a loss when Ron died that I wanted to send a message to others: that you need to treasure the time you have with each other.

Loss

The terrible depth of loss
When your life's partner
Passes on and you are left
To manage on your own,
All feelings, they just leave
And you are dazed
Beyond belief, to function
Just like a robot,
Thoughts and reason
Are no more,
For desire is not there
To carry on alone,
Then slowly, oh so slowly
Finally some semblance
Of life comes back again
To let you live as best you can.

"Loss"—It's how I felt after my husband's passing.

Vacations

The sights, the sounds erupt
As we enter into unknown spaces
We've not been to before,
Making vacations an adventure
To fill our curious mind,
What comes next, we wonder
On this journey that we're on,
So many things to enjoy
That piques our thirst to know
Of what's around the corner
When next we start to go,
On to the next section
We travel with delight,
Making all we've conquered
An entry in our memory bank
Of places that we've been.
We like to do things we hadn't done before
And it was like an adventure to find out what
Was around the corner.

Stormy Seas

Blackened sky with mottled clouds
That, to the naked eye, apparently
Control the roiling waters
Of the mighty ocean crashing
With a thunderous roar
Upon the rocky shore.
While Neptune's fist pounds relentlessly,
The sailor's landmark sends a beacon
To signal of the perils ever present,
As all vessels sail into port
Where safely they await
The calming of the storm,
And when the rage is over,
They venture back to sea
To face another day.

What Next?

With pen in hand
And paper ready,
What words will you put down?
It maybe solemn, sober words
Or ones that make no rhyme,
But whatever ones do come out,
They are your very own,
Leaving others to wonder at
What you will think up next.

It's Time to Say

I could not help but notice
How down you were today,
It seems the things
That count the most
Have wandered far away,
Now that all looks darkest
It's time to say a prayer
And soon you'll see
The darkness fade away.

Hello and Good-bye

There is a time to say hello
And then to say good-bye
No matter what goes between
You know whatever else
The love and understanding
Is what their memories will be
For that is what you gave to them
And they will all hold dear.

Journey of Choices

This journey that I'm taking now
Is not the one I want,
My love has gone home
To our Father up above,
Leaving me alone with
A choice that's not my own.

No one wants this choice.

Do You See?

Do you see what I see
When watching those around
The busy streets of town?
Some are shopping in the stores
While others walk about,
Now panhandlers do show up
Trying to survive
Misfortunes that came their way,
It makes me wonder
How each fits in
To the daily life I see,
It gives to me a chance
To appreciate the life
God gave to me.

Our Retirement

After fifty years of toiling
Our time has come
For relaxing as we wish.

We strived to thrive
Through thick and thin
So our leisure we could enjoy.

These changes that are taking place
Allow us to explore
So many things we'd like to do.

Other avenues of life I'm sure
Now retirement is here, shall
Give excitement to the twilight of our years.

Calm Home

While standing on the corner
Of the busy city street.

I watch some people pass on by
To their daily working place.

Soon the hustle of the traffic
Adds to the bustle of the day.

It drowns out shoppers looking
For good bargains of the day.

As I leave the area
And I reach my home again.

The peace that surrounds me
Does calm my shopping blues.

On Valentine's Day

A Valentine's Day should be
The time for you and me,
Sharing precious moments
That makes our time together
So fulfilling for each other,
There is not a day
To pass our way
That does not add
Another of those moments.

"On Valentine's Day"—we usually tried to do something special on this day.

Decisions

It's hard to see objectively
The task we have to do,
So many circumstances surround
Decisions to be made.

With heavy heart we feel our way
To make the wrong come right,
Do we, don't we, lend a hand
Or let fate have her way?

Deep within our conscience
With morals crying out,
The wrong must be corrected
And healed with steady times.

Inquiry for Meanings

Are there any reasons
    For doing what you do?
Are there any answers
    Why things do go awry?

As we search for meanings
    To the problems of the day,
The answers that we're looking for
    Should come forth right away.

But let us not a fool be
    And think they'll stay away,
For life is not an easy thing
    With problems every day.

A Spider's Web

I watched a spider weave a web
It's silk the finest in the land,
A lacy patch upon the branches
Of floral beauty that surround
The gardens near my home.

It weaves that web so easily
To survey the realm it's conquered,
Now when the foe does enter
Into the spider's home, it finds
The beauty that betrays.

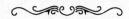

Just a Little Prayer

I wait by so patiently
To see you gain control
Of all the things
That trouble you
That don't want to let go.

As I watch and see
The changes taking place
I say a little prayer
Of thanks
For all I'm thankful for.

What Do You Do

What do you do
When your mind
Wanders far away?

What do you do
When control has gone astray
To places that cause stress?

It seems to be
An everlasting scheme
To bring about discomfort.

Challenging one's sanity
In all you say and do
To reach the point you ask

WHAT DO YOU DO?

"What Do You do" was written on one of those days when nothing seems to go right.

Picture Album

As we view our picture album,
The mountains that we saw
Are calling out to us.
It sets our senses tingling
And gives us such a rush,
Thinking of the time we had
While travelling through
The valleys and the hills.
With the air around so clear, it makes
Blue skies seem close enough to touch.

Off in the distance, a lone wolf
Howls to its mate
Somewhere near tree-lined ponds
That accent the countryside.
So when we stopped and listened
To nature's serenade,
We knew our dreams of repeating
That mountain trip of ours
Seemed not so far away.

Lifetime Memories

How pretty is the cover
Of the album on my knee?
As I open up the front, I wonder,
Do you see what I see
While looking through the book?
It is a glimpse of past times
Just sitting there before us—
A lifetime of memories.

The Evening Sky

The evening sky has darkened
With twinkling stars that shine like diamonds
In a prince's crown while ruling
The movement of the night.

I have the pleasure every eve
Of experiencing this grandeur
From my window
In seasons all the year.

Though nature does affect
The clarity at times,
I know the clouded blanket
Will not last all that long.

So as the eve approaches
Whether clear or covered up,
I know the stars are up there
And will rule every night.

Striking Rules

Morning dew is on the grass,
Little birds are calling out
As rays of the rising sun
Rouse sleeping neighborhoods,
The warming rays touch all
Of stirrings taking place
In sight of the regal sun
That rules from above.

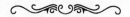

Success Achieved

Creating beauty all can see
A gift thought highly of
By everyone who has been touched
With a talent such as yours.

Long have you strived
To achieve success
And now the day has come
So now I say, take pride.

Be proud, for the best is yet to come
For this is the day that you
Have reached and gained
The credit you deserve.

"Success Achieved" is for my son and his wife. They are very talented and creative.

Time Together

Now that we've retired
Our time together has become
An exciting venture into a life
Of exploring those things
We couldn't do
When our family was around
So now that they are on their own
And living as they wish
It gives the freedom for what
We want to do.

Attitude of Gratitude

The attitude of gratitude can be
A blessing or a curse,
So many things affect
Our perception of the
Matter close at hand,
When we have done our very best
And received the appreciation of others,
Fullness to our life comes in knowing
We accomplished what we wanted,
Making gratitude a blessing
We are thankful for,
But when we try our hardest
Or at least we think we do,
The results that we expected
Can be not what we achieved,
For others do not see
What benefits there are,
And so our attitude becomes
An irritation we experience,
Then we struggle to gain control
To bring us back again
And make us realize
Our attitude should be
One we're thankful for when
We receive acceptance of rejection
In knowing others care.

"Attitude of Gratitude" is about how we see things and our reaction to them.

For You to Know

Why do we feel
The need to know
When it is not
Our place to know?

We are put here
On this earth
To do God's work
For the betterment of mankind.

The fight we have
Is against oppression
Of the freedom we enjoy
From our Savior up in Heaven.

Inspiration to Devastation

Wanting what's not yours
Can twist you inside out,
Wanting what's not yours
Is what the devil wants,
It brings to you distraction
Of all that is not right
And takes you where you
Should not be and into devastation,
So walk away and take control
Of everything you do
And don't let the devil
Be your constant guide
To rule your life with
The things you should not do.

I have seen too many people getting greedy and not being satisfied with what they are entitled to.

Clickety-Clack

Clickety-clack, clickety-clack
Train wheels passing by
On ribbons of steel to places
We dream about.

Exciting places so far away
Attracting our attention
When whistles blow, drawing us
To visit when we can.

The Blink of an Eye

With the blink of an eye,
Time passes us by
Into new tomorrows,
Ever onward, ever steadfast
The weeks, the days,
The hours, the minutes
Fade in an instant,
As nothing can hold Time
Pressing on in its quest.

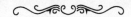

The Seasons of Our Life

Spring is birth of new life
As an infant we must be,
It's a time for growing
To see, to do all we can.

Summer is the time of developing
Into adults and all their ways,
Creating worlds within our grasp
To be the best we're meant to be.

Fall brings maturity
To use the talents given us,
Making the most of living
For the benefit of others.

Winter comes to all of us
For passing we must go,
Hopefully our legacy
Will bring peace to those behind.

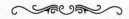

Remembrance Day

Sitting quietly on Remembrance Day
And thinking of the way we were,
One thought becomes so clear
Of the times that used to be,
It was the waiting
For my dad to come back from
The war that devastated
So many lives back then.

We were of the fortunate
To have him grace our lives,
For the years that followed
Those terrible years of strife,
So we should all listen
To the rumblings from the past
And strive to make this world
A place of harmony.

Then loved ones, friends, and neighbors
Won't have to go away
To settle those disruptions
That damage all our lives.

*"Remembrance Day"—I can remember waiting for my dad to come home
from the war. It was quite a few years later though that what war really
does to families really sank in.*

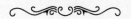

Tuning Breeze

The whisper of the breeze
As it passes by
Leaves one's feelings quite in tune
To a world that's ever changing
Each and every day.

Beautiful Voice

This life you lead
With care for family and friends
Will leave so many memories
To those who will remain.

Time passes by
And all can see
The warmth all feel
That you created.

And when you leave
As each must do
A void will be
That only time can heal.

Somewhere there is a new life
Your soul will enter into
One more beautiful
Than the one you made around you.

Special Friends

Special friends are rare indeed
Friendship not intruded on,
Just wholesome relations treasured dear,
Sharing, caring not what circumstances
Lead to difficulties unforeseen.

A helping hand placed openly
For all to see in time of need,
Heartfelt thanks and understanding
Make special friends like you
So rare indeed!

"Special Friends"—I'm blessed to have these people in my life.

Mother's Clock

My mother's clock upon the wall
Does constantly portray
The passing of each day,
On each hour we hear you call
To let us know when to say
It's time to work or time to play,
So as each day through time persists,
Your constant way will always exist.

Remember Not

Remember not the trying time
That Mother gave to you,
Remember not the heartaches
Of differences you had,
Remember not the pain and hurt
You suffered from her ways,
    For she is the one
        Who gave you life
    And the talents to create
        Special friendships, special gifts
    For all so fortunate
        To feel the strength you have
    In living each and every day
        With morals true and just
You cannot right the wrong
Or change the things gone by,
But please do thank the Lord above
For blessing her with you.

*"Remember Not"—Written for my neighbor who was losing her mom.
Mom was very miserable with everyone.*

Whatever Else

Whatever else you do today
Be sure to thank the Lord,
Whatever else does come along
Be sure to thank the Lord,
For He is always with you
In the good times and the bad,
So when you face each day
You know that you are covered
With His blessing from above,
    Just don't forget
    To thank the Lord
    For whatever comes your way.

A Walk in a Spring Bush

On this early spring day
We wandered through the bush
Where fallen leaves all dried and brown
Were rustling in the breeze,
The ground was becoming soft
Winter frost was leaving fast
As warm rays of sunshine beam down
From blue skies above.

As we followed trails
That led us to the cliffs, and
Basking in the sun,
Fresh air filled our lungs
Which left a peace that's deep within,
Lookouts allowed us to rest and
View the great expanse
That lay in solemn splendor
For the naked eye to see.

Little birds were out of sight
As protection they do need,
With turkey vultures soaring up above
They sought their sanctuary
In havens not far away,
The leaves on trees were sleeping yet
But nature soon will wake
And dress all foliage in
Custom colors that portray
The finest scenery.

Bring It Back to Him

Now that I'm alone
Without your company,
I find my time
Is empty as can be.
What should I do
To lighten up this load?
I'll try to find a place
That I can be
Of service to the Lord
By being all that
He would want for me.

Good-bye

We've come to say good-bye
To a dear one we all loved,
Who had such loving ways
And caring touch
That went deep down inside.
We will remember
Each one of us
Those things you did for us.
So now we're here to put to rest
The one that we all loved
With a fond farewell
And forever rest in peace.

Written for when my mother-in-law passed away.

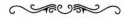

What Difference

What difference does the distance make
When we're near or far away?
The thought that you are with me
Will always bring me peace
And carry me wherever I'll be
To the safest place for me.

Cloud Pictures

Fluffy white clouds up in the sky
Making pictures as you pass by
Allowing one to drift away
To places just dreamed about.

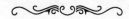

Finding Kinfolk

To be the only one for years
A sober thought indeed,
So many times a question asked
With answers not forthcoming,
It makes the joy of finding
Kinfolk so exciting.

To simply hope the quest will reach
An end to missing gaps,
Reflecting on events that brought
The joy of finding kin
A realization that life does
Sometimes give rewards.

Ron finally met his brother and sister a few years ago. They never knew about him, and it was like one of those stories you read about when it finally happened.

The Fact That I

The fact that I
Can plainly see
An article come forth
From places all around
Is just my talent
Brimming over.
I do believe deep down inside
Each person has a gift
For creation of some sort.
And so I hope
For each of you
That your talent
Emerges forth.

Desires

To fill a need of usefulness
One reaches deep inside
And brings forth one's ability
That creates a wondrous sight,
Fulfilling one's desires.

Calm

The calm that surrounds me
In the turmoil that's around
Is just what I do see
Of the precious gift
The Lord has give to have
Me survive the troubles
That come each and every day.

The Dancers

The rhythm of the dancers
As they float across the floor,
Graceful like a gliding swan
That graces a garden pond.

Whirling, swirling as they sail around
In harmony with the music,
A blur of color passing by
As together they make one.

Their nimble toes that barely touch
The floor beneath their feet
Make the dancers' fluid movements
Seem just like moving art.

This came to mind after watching a dance competition.

Katie

Eighty years you've lived on this earth
Given all with life's great zest,
Touching many that passed your way
With wisdom and kindness that are the best
Of humanity's gifts from God.

Helping others, you do so well
Easing burdens that come along,
When life's travels are intervened
By troubling times
We all have seen.

The many talents you've shown others
Make each of us admire
Those accomplishments that give us each
The drive to keep on going
When disruptions touch our lives.

Even now when illness touches you
You face that life in front of you,
Fighting illness to the end
And showing others that you don't give in
When the road ahead gets bumpy.

I know our family has been blessed
By the crossing of our paths,
So many times you've touched our lives
By the little things you do
Giving precious memories

When we think of you.

Katie was a very special lady who was like a surrogate mother for my daughter when she lived far away from me.

Spring

I see by the calendar
That spring is here at last
The winter snow is melting fast
And flowers have started growing.

I notice too the temperature is warming
Making longer days a pleasant thing
For winter-weary people waiting
To greet the days ahead.

Who

Who has the answers in this day and age
For problems not foreseen?
We do our best, at least we think we do,
To live by the Golden Rule.

And yet, misfortunes do occur
With seemingly no end,
To try our skills, our trust, our faith
In living by the Rule.

While little do we realize
That we are not true through.
If we stop to think about ourselves,
We'd know that yet we do our best.

It's not enough to pay the debt
Of our mistrustful soul,
Just stop and sit by yourself
Some unsuccessful day.

See if not one little best
Was not the best at all,
And then maybe, the best should be
To live by the Golden Rule.

The In-betweens

The ups, the downs,
The in-betweens
Are my daily life, you see,
It matters not
To the world outside
What goes inside of me,
For they did not
This addict make,
I did it by myself,
So now the challenge
Is to fight
And gain respect
Of the life that
I let go.

Written for a friend who works with addicts.

True Love

A love that lasts forever
Is deep and true indeed,
It means caring for the little things
That each attempt to do,
Sharing and caring
For all kinds of times
As they come along
With tenderness unending.

For my husband.

Signs of Winter

As I look around, I see
The signs of winter coming,
With leaves all falling to the ground
And flowers that stopped blooming,
The summer birds have flown south
As chilly air now nips at us,
It's into warmer clothes we go
To face the winter's coming,
So now's the time to polish up
The toys and tools that we need,
For fun and fitness to survive
Those snowflakes falling now,
Reminding us, our seasons change
With great diversity.

Country Evening

Listen to the rustle
Of the pine boughs gently swaying
To summer breezes passing through,
While quiet chirping dots the air
With soft harmony,
As darkening skies surround us
The quiet stillness calms
All bustling from the day,
Allowing tired bodies
The time to solve
One's anxiety of the day.

Our Pine Tree

The pine tree in our yard
Ever watchful standing there,
Little birds all flit about
On branches reaching out,
So now that you have grown
To dress up our backyard,
The daily pleasures we receive
From just you being there,
Gives a reason to say thanks
For nature's peaceful ways.

Me

When I think about
Just what I am,
A mixture I do see.
A wife and mother are the first,
As my family means the most.
I like to cook
No matter what,
But tasty it must be.
Other interests are my crafts,
And sewing's got to be
A priority, you see.
Now poetry has caught my eye,
A legacy, I guess.
Organizing, helping others, and
Volunteering too
Complete the mix that others see.

Spring's Arrival

The air's still crisp
But signs are there
For changes coming soon,
Snow is leaving
While through the ground
Spring flowers peek up through
Frozen soil that's giving way
To nature's changing way,
Soon returning birds of summer
Will herald all the rest
Of the springtime fast approaching.

Endless Pain

My heart does ache
When I do see
The pain you do endure
It isn't fair
That one so young
Suffer endlessly

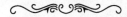

The Storm

Just when I think that all is calm
Another storm draws near,
With blackened clouds and thunderclaps
Shattering the air around us,
Now flashing bolts with jagged edge
An awesome sight to see,
Following winds and gusts so strong
It drives the rain into the ground,
Now when the storm comes to an end
The air is fresh, and all around,
Our world seems cleansed again.

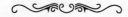

Hopefulness

I wonder if we shall ever see
A time of peace and tranquility,
Although all struggles carry on
Each answer can be found
If only bit by bit,
As each passing day
Gives up another piece
Of answers brought about
By patience and persistence,
Equality for all will undoubtedly
Be the end we all have sought.

Seeking Blessing

The time is now
To seek the Lord
When all seems lost,
Who else can bring
The peace that you are seeking?
Let each find their way
Among the troubles of the day,
To the peace the Lord does bring.

Evening in My Rocker

As I sit here, gently rocking,
With my tensions giving way
To a calm that is relaxing
The problems of the day,
Now that I've yielded
And my body is refreshed,
I find I have the strength
To meet another day.

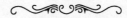

My Worth

You ask me, "What is your worth?"
Of this I cannot say,
For the things I do
I do for love and love alone,
What all you see me do
I hope you understand,
It was not for praise or glory
But in some small way
For the benefit of others,
So when I see that I have helped
In an ordinary way,
I know I did my best
Each and every day,
And that is why
I could not say
Just what my worth would be.

My Morning Cup of Coffee

The first thing in the morning
Before anything to be done,
My morning cup of coffee
Brings the start for things to come,
It helps me plan the day ahead
And organize my thoughts
To make my day successful
In this busy world of mine.

Written at my son's home when I was getting ready to help him make candles for his candle business.

I Remember

I remember the little girl
    You used to be
I remember the little girl
    Who often came to me
For caring ways and little needs
    That grandmas sometimes fill.

And through the years
    I watched you grow
To the woman you are now
    It fills my heart with pride
To see all that you've become
    Knowing that you're able to
Be the best that you can be.

This is for my granddaughters. I'm so proud of them all.

Autumn

Red, green, gold, and brown
Are colors of our Autumn
Adorning the world I see
From the window of my home
To comfort me when I am down.

As each passing day goes by
With trials all around
I need only to look upon
Such splendor that's provided by
Nature's majestic scenery
That softens all that's wrong.

Grain of Sand

Upon this earth we are
But a grain of sand to
The eternal day of God,
Mere souls to carry forth
His word to all
Who want to hear
Of love so great
No other can compare.

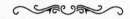

I look

I look and then I see
The wonder of His love
From little petals to mighty trees
The mountains and the seas
And greatness all around.

Who can wonder
How creative is His way
That gave us mighty scenes
To look upon each day?

Clouds Above

Darkened clouds are rolling in
Like armies on the march,
Distant rumbles fill the air
And lightning stabs the sky,
Now rain comes pouring in
On town and countryside.

May, 1956

The time as I remember
On that awful night when
That dreadful phone call came
To tell me of the possibility
That I may be a widow
And not see him again.

My heart sank deep
But I knew for sure
The reporter was mistaken
As I had talked to Ron
Earlier that night.

This was a very bad train wreck my husband was in, and he could have been killed but had changed places with the other trainman a few minutes before the accident. They had taken out a bridge when another train had pulled out in front of them.

Fly

Fly, fly, fly away
To a life you've never known,
How exciting the world becomes
When the chance comes
To fill your life
With adventures that are
A once-in-a-lifetime thing,
Enjoy and make the most
Of all you say and do
'Cause life is meant to be
Full of fun and freedom
To do the things that are to come,
So when you're aged
And you look back,
The memories that come to mind
Will fill ten thousand pages
With things that you have done.

Written for a granddaughter who was going to Germany to work for a year.

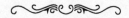

Greatness Above

A touch of blue comes peeking through
· The morning sky at dawn,
As daylight grows and fills our view
To nature all around,
We wonder what this day will bring
To fill our time upon this earth.

Smooth Transition

Mixed feelings as I look around
Of the happy times that happened here,
To see them slowly fade away
Brings a sadness deep inside.

I may not have lived here,
But on visits I was made to feel
The warmth that only families have
When caring for each related soul.

If I could I would
Ease the parting coming soon,
Hopefully I can achieve
A smooth transition to another place.

(June 23, 1994—one week, more or less, before Mom gave up her home of thirty-two years after Dad passed away.)

Mom had to give up her house after Dad died and came to live with me. It was really hard for her to give up her home, and I always felt she thought she was giving up her independence as well.

Printed in the United States
By Bookmasters